The Teacher Training Manual

Six Steps to Success in the Jewish Classroom

Lisa Bob Howard

Editorial Committee

Rabbi Steven Bob

Barbara L. Dragul

Lisa J. Goldstein

BEHRMAN HOUSE, INC.

www.behrmanhouse.com

BOOK AND COVER DESIGN: Randi Robin Design
PROJECT EDITOR: Terry S. Kaye

The publisher gratefully acknowledges the cooperation of the following
sources of photographs for this book: Congregation Etz Chaim,
Lombard, IL: front cover (middle), 61; Creative Image Photography: 8,
23, 38, 43, 48; Isaac M. Wise Temple, Cincinnati, OH: 21, 22; Richard
Lobell: 31; Ginny Twersky: front cover (left and right), back cover

Library of Congress Cataloging-in-Publication Data

Howard, Lisa Bob, 1978-
   The teacher's training manual : six steps to success in the jewish classroom /
Lisa Bob Howard.
      p. cm.
   ISBN 978-0-87441-811-8
1. Jewish religious education—Teacher training—Handbooks, manuals, etc.
2. Jewish religious education—Teaching methods—Handbooks, manuals, etc.
3. Jewish religious education of children—Handbooks, manuals, etc. I. Title.

   BM108.H72 2007
   296.6'8--dc22

                                                        2007012685

CONTENTS

Letter from the Author

Congratulations on becoming a Jewish teacher!
Teaching is inherently holy work, and Judaism has a long tradition
of holding teachers in the highest esteem.

This handbook will expand your understanding of children and
will help you build the skills you need to master the many roles of
a Jewish teacher. Each of the six chapters functions as a complete
workshop. You will discover what makes a Jewish classroom
distinctive, the different ways students learn, and how to include
students with learning differences. You will learn how to create a
master calendar, how to build dynamic bulletin boards, and how
to work effectively with *madrichim*. You will also learn the theory
of lesson planning, and you'll practice a variety of classroom
management techniques. Throughout, you will view the role of the
teacher through the lens of sacred text and reflect on how the lessons
in each chapter apply to your own classroom experience.

Teaching can be tremendously satisfying. I hope that as you take on
your teaching responsibilities, you find joy in working with your
students.

B'hatzlaḥah,

Lisa Howard

Why Be a Jewish Teacher?

By the end of this workshop, you will be able to:

► Name at least two opportunities that teaching in a religious school setting provides and two challenges that it presents.

► Describe at least three ways in which to create a Jewish classroom environment.

► Explain how you will incorporate Jewish values into your teaching.

► Describe how you will include family learning in your instruction.

Lesson Launch

Kol hakavod for becoming a religious school teacher! Teaching is inherently holy work, and Judaism has a long tradition of holding teachers in the highest esteem. That the Hebrew word *rav,* or rabbi, means "teacher" indicates that teaching is one of the most important functions of our community's leaders.

You undoubtedly have had many experiences and possess many strengths that will help you in your role as a religious school teacher. You may love children, be well organized, and have a deep knowledge of Jewish history and tradition. As you complete the workshops in this book and gain experience in the classroom, you will build on your strengths and gain new skills. Careful observation of and reflection on your students and your teaching will also enrich your professional development. In this first exercise, you will learn by reflecting on your surroundings.

Look around the room. What makes the environment distinctly Jewish? Consider decorations, ritual objects, books, and the people with whom you are sitting. Write your response on the lines below.

_____

_____

_____

_____

_____

_____

_____

_____

In this chapter, you will learn techniques for transforming your classroom into a Jewish environment. You will explore ways in which bulletin boards, your classroom management style, and the values you demonstrate can affect your students' Jewish learning. You will also learn how to expand your role as a teacher in order to reach your students' families so that the lessons taught in school can be reinforced at home.

THE GOALS OF RELIGIOUS SCHOOL EDUCATION

The goals of religious school education have changed over the years. In the 1950s, Hebrew schools aimed to teach Hebrew as well as Jewish history and holy texts as a supplement to religious practice in the home. With the increased secularization of American Jews, however, religious schools have become the primary place in which a great many Jewish children learn about Jewish rituals and traditions. Jewish religious schools often teach basic Jewish literacy, including the meaning of prayers and the rituals associated with prayers and holiday observance.

The three main goals of Jewish education are (1) enculturating Jewish children—transmitting to the next generation our people's history, rituals, practices, and values; (2) teaching basic Jewish skills, such as lighting Ḥanukkah candles, reciting Kiddush, and preparing for the Passover seder; and (3) providing Jewish students with the experience of actively participating in the Jewish community.

UNIQUE TEACHING OPPORTUNITIES

Teaching in a religious school provides unique opportunities that distinguish the profession of the religious school teacher from that of the secular school teacher. Jewish educators teach subjects in which values are an explicit part of the curriculum. Their focus is the meaning and joy of being Jewish. And they are part of a larger community with the shared purpose of passing Judaism on to the next generation.

A CHALLENGING ENVIRONMENT

As a religious school educator, you will face a unique set of challenges, including students whose attention and energy have been drained by their secular school studies, students whose attendance is spotty as a result of commitments to sports and other activities, and in some instances students who just lack the motivation to learn.

Brainstorm to come up with a list of other opportunities and challenges in teaching religious school. Note them on this chart.

Opportunities	Challenges

Share two or three of the items from your list with your colleagues. On a flipchart or the chalkboard, create a master list of the ideas you shared. Then together choose one or two challenges, and discuss possible solutions. Choose one or two opportunities, and explore strategies for taking advantage of them. Record your thoughts in response to these prompts:

Challenges: _____

_____

_____

Solutions: _____

_____

_____

Opportunities: _____

_____

_____

Strategies: _____

_____

_____

Creating a Jewish Environment

The Real World

A few minutes before the start of her third-grade religious school class, Ms. Cohen walked around her classroom to make sure everything was in order for the day's lesson. Most of her students had already arrived. A few were sitting on the floor, playing a Jewish board game. Several were writing brief descriptions for a bulletin board display of mitzvot that they had performed during the week. Others were chatting as they sorted through a collection of Jewish storybooks, looking for books to borrow for the week. A few students were at their desks, working together on a holiday word-search puzzle. By the time the bell rang to signal the start of class, almost every student was engaged in some form of Jewish learning.

This picture of Ms. Cohen's class exemplifies ways in which informal Jewish learning can take place in the religious school classroom. By providing an assortment of Jewish games, displaying bulletin boards that celebrate Jewish values, and offering a selection of Jewish books, you can create a physical environment that is distinctly Jewish. For some of your students, your classroom will be the primary place in which they experience Jewish culture, so it is important to create a positive atmosphere for Jewish learning and living.

Here are other ways in which to create a Jewish environment in your classroom:

▶ *Display a tzedakah box prominently,* and encourage students to give tzedakah weekly.

▶ At the beginning of each class, *recite the prayer for studying Torah (". . . la'asok b'divrei Torah").* Say the appropriate blessings any time the class eats or drinks together.

▶ *Provide Jewish worksheets, games, puzzles, and books* that students can use if they come to class early or finish an assignment before their classmates.

▶ *Have students create Hebrew labels for objects in the room.* If your students have not yet learned to write Hebrew, ask your principal if students in an upper-level class might create the labels for you, or use a Hebrew typesetting program to make them yourself.

► *Create interactive bulletin boards that support your curriculum.* You will learn more about creating bulletin boards in Workshop 2. Your principal and local resource center are also good sources of bulletin board inspiration.

► *Hang Jewish posters on the walls.* Make sure that when students' eyes wander during class, they see Jewish holiday scenes, ritual objects, Hebrew words, and/or a map of Israel.

► *Play Jewish or Israeli music* as students enter the classroom and do work at their seats. Play upbeat songs at the start of class and softer, less distracting music while students are working at their seats.

At the beginning of this workshop, you listed the aspects of your learning space that make it feel Jewish. Look back at that list, and consider whether you can now think of other Jewish elements that you might incorporate into your classroom. Write any additional ideas on these lines:

_____

_____

_____

_____

_____

Teaching with Jewish Values

One of the best ways in which to create a Jewish environment in your classroom is by promoting Jewish values. Creating a classroom culture in which *midot* (Jewish virtues) are celebrated will help strengthen your classroom community. Award *derech eretz* (appropriate behavior) points to students when they demonstrate appropriate classroom behavior, such as treating classmates with respect, talking politely, and following classroom rules. Create a *derech eretz* chart, and use stickers, stars, or checkmarks to track each student's points. Make the points redeemable for small prizes, such as a few minutes of free time, colored pencils, or bite-size pieces of candy (if your school allows). You might also reward students with a privilege, such as choosing a class activity. By making *derech eretz* a regular part of your students' school day, you will continually reinforce this important Jewish value.

You might also promote Jewish values by organizing a class tzedakah project. Collecting food for a shelter, beautifying the synagogue, gathering the class together to call a sick classmate, or organizing a day on which to work for a local service organization—all of these activities build community while reinforcing Jewish values in a practical way.

In addition to teaching *about* Jewish values and having your students put them into practice, aim to *serve as* a Jewish role model by incorporating Jewish values into your teaching. Treat students with *kavod* (respect), and insist that they treat you and one another in the same manner. Here are some ways in which to model the value of *kavod:*

▶ Be friendly, but do not try to be your students' friend.

▶ Take your students' opinions, questions, and ideas seriously.

▶ Make only those promises that you can and will fulfill.

▶ Do not raise your voice no matter how badly your students behave.

▶ Address specific behaviors when expressing disapproval.

▶ Do not speak sarcastically; do not tease or demean your students.

▶ Treat your students equally and fairly.

▶ Be credible. If a student asks a question you cannot answer, be honest about your uncertainty. Talk to your principal or rabbi, or do research to find the answer.

Another way to use Jewish values to guide your teaching is by creating classroom rules based on values such as *derech eretz, kavod, shalom* (peace), *lo levayesh* (not embarrassing others), *raḥmanut* (compassion), and *tikun olam* (repairing the world). Post these values on a bulletin board, and refer to them when you praise or correct a student's behavior.

Working with your colleagues in a small group, list two to four other ways in which you might promote Jewish values in your class.

Family Learning

Family education is an essential component of successful Jewish education. As the following scenario demonstrates, engaging parents in family learning can help students make connections between what they learn in school and what their family practices and values. When lessons are reinforced at home, their meaning is enhanced immensely.

The Real World

Mr. Katz's fifth-grade curriculum focuses on Jewish heroes. At the beginning of the year, Mr. Katz sent home a letter asking parents to help their children identify a family member or close family friend who might be considered a Jewish hero, someone who demonstrates important Jewish values, such as *tikun olam*, *tzedek* (justice), and *piku'aḥ nefesh* (saving a life). Over the course of the year, students are to interview their heroes, gather information about the mitzvot their heroes have performed, and present their heroes' stories in class. Through this project, Mr. Katz's students make connections between the lessons they are learning in class and their family's values. Parents are engaged throughout the year too.

One of the challenges facing religious school teachers is that their students' parents are often unfamiliar with the material their children are learning. By keeping parents informed of classroom activities and providing them with adult-level resources on the topics you teach, you can help them continue their children's Jewish education at home.

The following ideas can help you engage parents and other family members in the content of your classes.

▶ *Create a monthly newsletter or a Web page.* Students might write articles about what they have learned, or you might write a summary of the lessons you have covered in the past month. For the most efficient delivery, e-mail the newsletter to your students' parents.

▶ *Assign family discussion questions that relate to each lesson.* Use the answers in your lessons. For example, if your class is studying the Ma'ariv Aravim, a prayer that praises God for creating the evening, have students ask their parents and siblings to describe the most memorable sunset they have experienced.

► *Invite parents to class for special performances or presentations,* for example, a play based on the week's Torah portion or an exhibition of art projects relating to an upcoming holiday. Try to add two or three parents' days to your class calendar.

► If you are teaching younger students, *ask parents to volunteer to read a story to the class.* Ask the parent to pick out a Jewish book that he or she would like to share, or recommend one yourself.

► *Encourage children to check out books from the classroom or school library* to read at home with their parents.

► *Send home a list of Web sites* that provide adult-level information about the topics your students are studying in class.

Focus on Text

וְשִׁנַּנְתָּם לְבָנֶיךָ.

You shall teach them diligently to your children.

—Deuteronomy 6:7

Recited daily as part of the V'ahavta prayer, these words from the Book of Deuteronomy represent an important Jewish tradition. Read narrowly, the commandment directs parents to teach their children the words of the Torah. It can also be understood as charging all Jews with the task of passing Judaism to the next generation.

As a Jewish teacher, you can fulfill this biblical directive by making parents your partners in their children's religious school education. Encourage parents to read Jewish books with their children, have students create a Shabbat kit for their family, send home worksheets and activities to be completed by the family, or choose one of the other ideas presented in this workshop. Through these efforts, you can help parents become their children's Jewish teachers.

Create a *brit,* an agreement, between parents and teachers that outlines the roles of each in a child's Jewish education. Describe an ideal partnership between parents and teachers:

Parents agree to _____

_____

Teachers agree to _____

_____

Reflections

Reflection through journaling is a proven way for teaching professionals to improve their teaching skills. In his book *The Courage to Teach: Exploring the Inner Landscape of a Teacher's Life,* Parker J. Palmer explains that in addition to learning what to teach and how to teach, educators should explore how their own interests and ideas affect their teaching style and methods.

Consider spending a few minutes journaling after each class. Reflect on what worked well, what did not go as planned, what successful strategies you will repeat, and what you will do differently in the future. You might also make notes about those students who made progress and those about whom you are concerned.

Use the space below for your first reflection. If your school year has already begun, describe what is working well and what challenges you are facing. If your school year has not yet begun, describe what you are looking forward to and what, if anything, is making you apprehensive. Use an additional sheet of paper if necessary.

Planning for a Great Year

Objectives

By the end of this workshop, you will be able to:

▶ Describe how you will set up your classroom for the new school year.

▶ List at least three systems you will implement to help your class run smoothly.

▶ Prepare a plan for the first day of school.

▶ Describe how you will effectively engage and use your *madrich* or *madrichah* (teacher's aide).

Lesson Launch

Think of an event in your life that required a great deal of planning. Perhaps it was a wedding, a trip, or a move to a new home. You may have made lists, diagrams, or spreadsheets to organize the event. Which strategies worked well for you? Which did not?

_____

_____

_____

_____

Teaching requires careful planning. Before the school year starts, you should plan how you will implement your curriculum, set up your room, and welcome your students on their first day. Throughout the year, you should map out lessons and assessments. This workshop will guide you through the process of planning for the school year.

CREATING A MASTER CALENDAR FOR THE TEACHING YEAR

Planning your curriculum for the year might seem like an overwhelming task. You may have been given a textbook or two that you are expected to have your students complete, or you may have been given curricular objectives to attain. How will you know how much time to spend on each topic? Too many teachers simply begin teaching from the beginning of their textbook or curriculum outline without considering how they should pace their teaching. Map out your year so that you cover your curriculum, finish your textbook, and still have time for special projects, family days, field trips—even snow days!

Step 1: Prepare

▶ How many times this year is your class scheduled to meet? _____

▶ How many chapters does your textbook contain? _____

▶ Divide the number of chapters by the number of class sessions to determine the approximate number of class sessions to spend on each chapter. Write the result here: _____

Look through your textbook and the suggestions in the teacher's guide to determine whether some chapters will require more time than others.

Step 2: Plan

On your school calendar, mark the following:

▶ the start and end of the school year

▶ vacation days

▶ days on which special activities are planned, such as a field trip or a family learning program

▶ Jewish and national holidays

To help pace your teaching, note the topics and/or the textbook chapters that you will cover during each class. Doing this will help you decide how much time to devote to each topic.

Step 3: Revise

Keep in mind that your master calendar will evolve during the year. Your principal may schedule a special program for your class, school may be canceled due to bad weather, or a unit of study may take longer than you expected. Include two or three "flex" days when you can catch up on your curriculum or do special projects that had not made it onto your original plan.

SETTING UP YOUR CLASSROOM

The setup of your room establishes the tone of your class. Even if your room is used by another teacher on a different day or by an early childhood class in the morning, consider the following when arranging your room.

- ▶ **Seating.** If you plan to have students work in groups, consider arranging the desks in clusters, or if possible, forgo desks in favor of tables at which students can work in groups. If your lessons will be based on discussion, consider setting up the desks in a semicircle so that students can see one another. Also consider how you will assign seats. Many religious school teachers allow students to choose their own seats each week; others prefer to assign seats for the year and create a corresponding seating chart.

- ▶ **The teacher's desk.** Although you will not spend much time at your desk while you are teaching, you will most likely need it for storing and organizing books, handouts, and supplies. Place your desk at the front of the room. That way it can serve as a focal point should you want your students to direct their attention toward you.

- ▶ **A learning center.** Consider creating an area in the room for Jewish games, Hebrew books, enrichment worksheets, and/or Jewish music—a place where students can engage in self-directed learning if they arrive early or finish an activity before their classmates.

- ▶ **Storing supplies.** You will need a place to keep pencils, markers, extra textbooks, and other supplies. So that classroom supplies are well organized and accessible, store them in clearly labeled bins or drawers or on shelves. Also consider where snacks will be kept and served and where students will place coats, backpacks, and any other items they bring to class.

- ▶ **Interior decoration.** How will you make your classroom feel warm and inviting to your students? You might, for example, strategically arrange posters, books, and puzzles so that students are motivated to explore them. In addition, create a place to hang students' work and photographs of class activities so that students come to feel that the room is truly theirs.

CREATING DYNAMIC BULLETIN BOARDS

Interactive bulletin boards are a good way to create a Jewish environment in your classroom, and they can also serve as a wonderful teaching tool. There are many types of interactive bulletin boards; three types are described here.

Sequencing boards. Choose a story or prayer, divide it into parts, and challenge students to arrange the parts in the correct order on a sequencing board. For example, write or print out each word of a prayer on an index card. Attach the index cards to a bulletin board with pushpins or reusable adhesive putty. Post the words in the correct order so that students can practice reading the prayer; remove one word, and have students identify it; or scramble the words, and have students put them in the proper order. Bible stories, descriptions of rituals, and historical events can all be taught with a sequencing board.

Choose a topic you will be teaching in the next few weeks, and describe how you might use a sequencing board in your lesson.

_____

_____

_____

Sorting boards. Challenge students to sort pictures into categories on a sorting board. For example, create a holiday sorting board for first-graders with pictures of Ḥanukkah and Passover objects and foods. Divide the bulletin board into two columns, one labeled "Ḥanukkah" and one labeled "Passover." Have students sort and post the cards as a class, or distribute the cards to the class and invite each student to place his or her card in the correct column.

Describe how you might use a sorting board in your class.

_____

_____

_____

Tracking boards. Bulletin boards that expand throughout the year can help you connect new concepts to previously taught lessons. You might, for example, create a time line. As the class studies historical events, use words and pictures to represent them on the time line. The growth of a tracking board is a great visual reminder of how much the class has learned. Tracking boards can be used to reinforce holiday lessons, the prayers in a service, Hebrew words with a common root, or the beliefs and practices of the different movements of Judaism.

Describe how you might use a tracking board in your class.

_____

_____

_____

Creating Systems for Success

Organized systems help the school day flow smoothly. Procedures like collecting tzedakah, taking attendance, cleaning up the classroom, and lining up students at the door will proceed more efficiently if you have systems in place.

Assigning students to assist you with regular activities can help you accomplish your many tasks and will encourage students to think of themselves as leaders in the classroom. For elementary school students, create a job board with roles such as "materials handler," "timekeeper," "cleanup captain," "attendance monitor," and "messenger." Make sure the process for assigning jobs is simple so that you can change assignments regularly.

Many teachers also use rewards systems, such as the one described in the following scenario, to motivate students to follow directions, stay on task, apply themselves to their work, and exhibit good behavior.

The Real World

Jason, a *madrich* in a fourth-grade classroom, is in charge of the class sticker system. When he sees students helping each other, working diligently, or cleaning up without being asked, he awards them stickers to put on their folders. When a student has earned five stickers, he or she may show the folder to Jason, who will allow the student to choose a small prize, such as an eraser or a piece of candy. Students often go out of their way to do things that will earn them stickers.

Stickers work well for elementary-school students. For older students, consider awarding points to the class as a whole. After the class earns, say, twenty-five points, reward students with a party or allow them to take turns assuming the role of teacher for part of a day.

You also need to establish procedures to start lessons. Consider starting each class with a "sponge activity"—an activity that soaks up time when students first come in or when you are busy with administrative tasks, like taking attendance and collecting tzedakah. Use sponge activities to review lessons. For example, ask students to recall three things they learned during the last class session. You can also use sponge activities to introduce the day's lesson. If you are teaching about Havdalah, for example, you might display a spice box and ask students to list as many words as they can to describe it. Word-search puzzles, riddles, and rebus stories can all serve as quick and easy sponge activities.

Choose a daily classroom activity, and describe a system you might implement to carry it out smoothly.

_____

_____

_____

_____

Working with Madrichim

The Real World

The second-graders used to trickle into class late, but no longer. The teacher asked Leah, a *madrichah*, to begin a game about ten minutes before each class. During that time, the teacher finished setting up the room and talked to the parents who accompanied their children to the classroom. The students were so eager to participate in Leah's games that the tardiness soon ceased.

Madrichim can be a great help in your class if you give them effective assignments. They can work one-on-one with students, set up art projects and snacks, manage administrative tasks, and even teach mini-lessons. The following suggestions can help you work successfully with a *madrich* or *madrichah*.

1. **Tap into talents.** At an orientation meeting, ask your *madrich* or *madrichah* about his or her extracurricular activities and hobbies. Think about how you can put those interests to work in the classroom. For example, a *madrich* who is active in drama may be able to direct the students in a short play. A *madrichah* with an interest in art might create bulletin boards, develop holiday art projects, or illustrate handouts.

2. **Define responsibilities.** Determine what tasks your *madrich* or *madrichah* will be responsible for in each class session (perhaps collecting tzedakah and/or taking attendance) and what tasks he or she will be responsible for as needed (perhaps leading groups or creating bulletin boards). For a fuller list, consult *The Madrichim Manual* by Lisa Bob Howard (Behrman House), a handbook for *madrichim*.

Tasks that *madrichim* might perform are listed below.

Administrative Tasks	Interactive Tasks	Creative Tasks
• Set up the classroom. • Take attendance. • Collect tzedakah. • Distribute handouts. • Set up snacks. • Correct students' work. • Manage incentive charts. • Set up supplies. • Reorganize the classroom at end of day.	• Greet students as they enter the classroom. • Escort younger students to the bathroom. • Help students with art projects. • Help students with class work. • Lead students in small-group activities. • Manage transitions between activities. • In consultation with you, plan, create, and teach mini-lessons. • Read stories to the class. • Work one-on-one with students who need help.	• Create bulletin boards. • Create models for art projects.

3. **Share a copy of your lesson plan.** A *madrich* or *madrichah* will be better able to assist you and your students if he or she has seen the lesson plan. For example, if your *madrich* knows that you have planned an art project, he can make sure there are enough scissors, markers, and other supplies.

4. Allow *madrichim* to teach. When *madrichim* teach mini-lessons, they are training to become members of the next generation of Jewish educators. The experience will help them develop leadership and classroom-management skills. Although you may not want to give up control of an activity, consider what you can gain by allowing *madrichim* to teach: The experience affords you a wonderful opportunity to observe how your students interact and learn.

The following activities can introduce *madrichim* to the art of teaching:

► *Read a story to the class.* Reading stories aloud allows *madrichim* to gain comfort in the role of teacher. *Madrichim* who are already at ease in front of the class may also lead students in an activity relating to the story. For example, they might have students design new covers for the book or illustrate their favorite scene.

► *Lead a game. Madrichim* may lead an educational game that they have seen you lead.

► *Present a how-to lesson.* Teaching a how-to lesson allows *madrichim* to break a skill into manageable components and demonstrate them a step at a time. For example, *madrichim* might teach students to write Hebrew letters, light Ḥanukkah candles, or braid a ḥallah.

5. Create a contract. A contract between a teacher and a *madrich* or *madrichah* will ensure that they share expectations and an understanding of their responsibilities. Refer to *The Madrichim Manual,* page 15, for an easy-to-use contract.

The First Day of School

Both teachers and students feel nervous and excited about the first day of school. To help your students feel at ease in your classroom, greet them at the classroom door. Use the first day to start to get to know your students—and their names!—and share your expectations for the year. Plan one or two mixer activities to help everyone feel comfortable in class. Classmate bingo is a popular and effective choice, as it gets everyone up and talking. Fill in each square of a bingo chart with a characteristic that is likely to describe several students in the class—for example, "has a pet," "likes to read," and "knows ten letters of the Hebrew alphabet." Instruct students to find someone that each square describes, using each classmate's name only once (or twice, depending on the number of squares and the size of the class).

In addition to mixer activities, you will want to spend time going over class rules, policies, and procedures. As you learned in Workshop 1, it is important to use the classroom to teach students about *derech eretz*. Some teachers simply tell students the rules, but a more effective method is to work with the class as a community to create a "class covenant." Phrase the rules you come up with in a positive way. Rather than "No interrupting," for example, lead students to come up with "Listen respectfully to others." You will learn more about rules and other classroom management techniques in Workshop 4.

It is also important to teach content on the first day: a story, a concept, or a skill that will get students excited about the work they will be doing in your class and provide them with a constructive answer when their parents ask, "What did you learn on your first day of religious school?"

FIRST-DAY CHECKLIST

To ensure that you are fully prepared for the school year, complete the following items before the first day of school.

☐ Review textbooks and teacher's guides.

☐ Establish communication with parents by means of an introductory letter or phone call.

☐ Familiarize yourself with the school's emergency procedures.

☐ Meet your *madrich* or *madrichah,* and define his or her role in the classroom.

☐ Review your class roster and familiarize yourself with your students' names.

☐ Find out whether any students have special needs, such as learning differences or physical disabilities.

☐ Memorize or post the class schedule so that you know what time your students must be at *t'filah,* music class, or any other special activities.

☐ Create systems for tracking attendance, collecting tzedakah, checking homework, reorganizing the classroom, and other routine tasks.

☐ Set up your room (refer to the discussion in this workshop on "Setting Up Your Classroom").

☐ Be sure that you have pencils, paper, art supplies, and textbooks for every student.

☐ Plan several extra activities to do with your students if your lessons take less time than you expected.

☐ Prepare sponge activities for students to work on if they arrive early or finish their work ahead of their classmates.

☐ Create a folder for substitute teachers, including the class roster, the lesson plan, the schedule, and classroom policies.

Focus on Text

וְדִבַּרְתָּ בָּם בְּשִׁבְתְּךָ בְּבֵיתֶךָ וּבְלֶכְתְּךָ בַדֶּרֶךְ וּבְשָׁכְבְּךָ וּבְקוּמֶךָ.

*Speak about them when you stay at home and when you are away,
when you lie down and when you rise up.*

—Deuteronomy 6:7

Workshop 2

This text, a continuation of the verse that you studied in Workshop 1, instructs us to be mindful of the laws of the Torah at all times. It suggests that Jewish learning and practice should extend beyond the synagogue and the religious school. Being a Jewish teacher gives you the opportunity to teach meaningful lessons that deeply affect your students' lives. The educators Jay McTighe and Grant Wiggins suggest that teachers should identify enduring understandings—the lessons that they want their students to retain after they have forgotten most of the details. The enduring understandings are the concepts in your curriculum that have value beyond the classroom, that you hope students will be mindful of when they are at home and when they are away. Enduring understandings in a religious school classroom might include an appreciation of Jewish values, the feeling that one is connected to Jewish history, a love of Israel, or an understanding of the importance of the Hebrew language.

List four enduring understandings specific to your curriculum. As you plan the setup of your room, the content of bulletin boards, and the activities and special projects that your class will engage in, keep these enduring understandings in mind.

1. _____

_____

2. _____

_____

3. _____

_____

4. _____

_____

25

Reflections

Describe three practical steps you will take to prepare for the school year in each of the following areas:

1. Creating a master calendar.

   a.

   b.

   c.

2. Setting up the classroom.

   a.

   b.

   c.

3. Planning for the first day.

   a.

   b.

   c.

4. Working with a *madrich* or *madrichah*.

   a.

   b.

   c.

Creating Effective and Engaging Lessons

Lesson Launch

Complete this sentence. Then, share your response with your colleagues.

A good lesson is like a good book because it _____

_____

_____.

In this workshop, you will learn how to create lessons that capture your students' interest, keep them engaged, teach them something new, and offer a satisfying conclusion. You will learn about the traditional model of lesson planning, which teachers have long used successfully, and about Understanding by Design, an innovative approach that many educators now prefer.

The Traditional Model

The traditional model of lesson planning consists of instructional objectives, a set induction and a variety of activities that support the objectives, assessments, and a conclusion that measures the objectives' success and draws the lesson to a close.

Step 1: Develop Instructional Objectives

Instructional objectives are precise statements that describe what you intend to teach. Specifying objectives will help you create lessons that meet your goals and determine whether you have met them.

Dr. Robert Mager, an expert in creating instructional objectives, explains that the best objectives use language that precisely articulates what students will be able to do at the end of a lesson. You might want students to be able to *describe, read,* or *list* information—or *summarize, identify,* and *write.* Avoid words such as *know* and *understand.*

For Mager, precise and effective objectives include measurable performance criteria that detail how well students should be able to execute the tasks. The objectives at the beginning of each workshop in this book exemplify Mager's principles, as do these:

> ▶ Students will be able to read V'ahavta with fewer than four mistakes.

> ▶ On an unlabeled map of Israel, students will be able to identify three cities and two bodies of water.

> ▶ Students will be able to recount the Purim story in their own words.

Practice writing instructional objectives that meet the criteria described above. Write a sample objective for each of the following lessons.

1. An introductory lesson on the Sh'ma for first-graders:

_____

_____

2. A lesson about Jacob's marriages to Rachel and Leah for fifth-graders:

_____

_____

3. A history lesson about the Six Day War for ninth-graders:

_____

_____

Step 2: Create a Set Induction

The set induction, or motivational introduction, should capture students' attention and help them develop an emotional connection to the content of the lesson. Good set inductions prepare students to learn. They also set the tone for the rest of the day's activities. In this book, the Lesson Launch serves as a set induction for each workshop.

Set inductions use a "hook" to stimulate students' interest and relate the day's topics to their experiences. The following hook activities can be used with a variety of lessons:

- ▶ Play a clip of a movie or a song that relates to the lesson.
- ▶ Ask students to share stories from their experience. For example, ask them to tell about a journey they once took (for a lesson about Abraham) or a disagreement they had with a sibling (for a lesson about Jacob and Esau).
- ▶ Display ritual objects—for example, a *ḥanukkiyah* and candles for a lesson on the Ḥanukkah blessings or a spice box for a lesson on Havdalah.

After presenting the hook activity, explain what the class will be learning, and present your objectives for the lesson. Consider writing an abbreviated version of the objectives on the board.

Write a set induction for one or two topics that you will be teaching in the next few weeks.

_____

_____

_____

_____

_____

Step 3: Create Activities

Activities make up the bulk of a lesson. Each activity in a lesson should support one (or more) of the instructional objectives; its purpose and meaning should be clearly identifiable. You will learn more about creating activities later in this workshop.

Step 4: Develop Assessments

To determine whether your students are retaining the skills and information you teach each week, incorporate a variety of assessments into your lessons. Some assessments are done informally, by observation and verbal exchange. Others are done formally, with quizzes, worksheets, and presentations.

Assessments are an essential tool for lesson planning. Whenever possible, use authentic assessments—assessments that allow students to apply new skills to real-life situations. For example, to determine how well students can read the blessings in the Havdalah service, instead of having them read aloud from their textbooks or a prayer book, have them lead a class Havdalah service. Other examples of authentic assessments include performing rituals, participating in debates, creating portfolio collections, performing skits, and giving oral presentations.

List four ways in which you might assess your students' progress.

1._____

2._____

3._____

4._____

Step 5: Provide Closure

Just as you should begin each lesson with an introduction in the form of a set induction, you should end each lesson with a closure activity. A closure should summarize what students have learned, reconnect the lesson to their experiences, and set the stage for homework or future lessons on the topic. One effective and easy closure activity that can be adapted to almost any lesson is the "ticket out." In this activity, each student shares one new thing he or she learned that day or one question still outstanding—without repeating any other students' responses. This activity gives students the opportunity to summarize what they have learned, thereby providing you with an assessment of their learning.

Other closure activities include making a poster summarizing the main points of a lesson, journaling (as in the Reflections section of each workshop in this book), and playing a simple review game. Earlier in this workshop, you created set inductions for one or two lessons you will be teaching. On the lines below, develop closure activities for the same lesson or lessons.

_____

_____

_____

_____

Understanding by Design

In Workshop 2, you learned about the importance of focusing on enduring understandings—those insights, understandings, and values that students should retain after the details of individual lessons have faded from memory. Jewish education aims to help students find personal meaning in Judaism, form a Jewish identity, and live according to Jewish values. Understanding by Design, the innovative approach to lesson planning created by Grant Wiggins and Jay McTighe, is particularly useful for Jewish schools because of its focus on teaching big ideas, or enduring understandings, that students retain beyond the classroom.

Wiggins and McTighe advocate a three-step process for creating meaningful lessons. Using this method, known as backward design, teachers first identify the big ideas, or enduring understandings, in the topic they are teaching. They then determine how they will measure students' understanding of these ideas. Finally, they create activities designed to help students achieve the desired results.

Step 1: Identify Desired Results

The first step in creating lessons using the Understanding by Design model is to consider what aspect of the lesson you want to endure. For the content you are teaching, consider what is important to know and do. If you are teaching the Shabbat candle-lighting ritual, for example, you might decide that students should know why two or more candles are lit on Shabbat, how to recite the blessing in Hebrew, and the order in which the ritual is performed.

Beyond those pragmatic lessons, students should gain the enduring understanding that lighting Shabbat candles connects them to Jews all over the world and creates a distinctly holy time in an otherwise secular week.

In the Understanding by Design model, teachers create essential questions rather than instructional objectives. Essential questions lead students to learn through inquiry, an approach that deepens understanding. Understanding by Design lesson plans should include one to three open-ended, thought-provoking questions that encompass your proposed enduring understandings. The following essential questions are appropriate for a religious school class:

▶ What is the purpose and meaning of prayer?

▶ Why is Israel important to American Jews? What are my responsibilities toward the State of Israel?

▶ What does the story of the Flood teach us about the relationships among God, human beings, and animals?

Write one to three essential questions for the enduring understandings presented in the Shabbat candle-lighting example.

_____

_____

_____

_____

Step 2: Determine Acceptable Evidence

In the second step, teachers determine how they will know that students have acquired the knowledge and skills necessary to answer the key questions of the lesson. The most meaningful assessments are performance tasks—real-life applications of knowledge and skill. These are similar to the authentic assessments that are used in the traditional model of lesson planning. For the lesson about lighting Shabbat candles, for example, you might test students' understanding of the big idea of creating holy Jewish time by having them write poems or short essays about Shabbat. You might then encourage them to read their compositions to their family before lighting Shabbat candles at home.

Step 3: Plan Learning Experiences

Understanding by Design promotes lessons that are not only engaging but also meaningful and effective. The activities you choose should support the material to be learned that you identified in the first two steps of the backward design process. You will learn more about creating effective and engaging lessons in the next section.

Activities That Engage and Teach

No matter which method of lesson planning you use, the activities you create should directly support your instructional objectives or essential questions. Purposeful activities should lead students to meet the goals you set and answer the essential questions of the lesson. Such activities are likely to be successful because students will perceive their purpose and therefore engage in them more willingly.

Activities should vary from week to week. As we will discuss in more detail in Workshop 5, students learn in different ways. Using a variety of teaching techniques will increase the likelihood of your reaching every student. In addition, varying teaching techniques helps keep students engaged. You might adapt the following activities to meet the needs of your classroom:

Writing Activities

- ▶ Create a class newspaper.
- ▶ Write a letter to a biblical or historical figure.
- ▶ Write a journal entry from the point of view of a biblical or historical figure.
- ▶ Compose a poem.
- ▶ Create a travel brochure.
- ▶ Make up new lyrics to a song.
- ▶ Create a word-search or crossword puzzle.
- ▶ Additional ideas: _____

Arts Activities

- ▶ Create a Jewish ritual object.
- ▶ Design and make scenery for a class play.
- ▶ Design an advertisement.
- ▶ Paint a mural to hang on a wall of the classroom.
- ▶ Illustrate a story.
- ▶ Make a scrapbook recalling the life of a biblical or historical figure.
- ▶ Additional ideas: _____

Movement Activities

► Learn an Israeli dance.

► Perform a short play. (There are several excellent Jewish plays for children, including Stan J. Beiner's *Sedra Scenes: Skits for Every Torah Portion* and Richard J. Allen's *Parashah Plays for Children of All Ages,* both from ARE, an imprint of Behrman House.)

► Play a movement-based game, such as Simon Says in Hebrew.

► Reenact or stage a debate or a trial.

► Play charades.

► Additional ideas: _____

_____

Methods of Presentation

In addition to varying the type of activities you use, vary your method of presentation. Alternate among frontal teaching, group work, discussion, and individual seat work to keep students engaged and to accommodate different types of learners.

Most classes incorporate some **frontal teaching,** in which the teacher is the focus of the class's attention, such as in a lecture, recounting a story, or explaining a concept. This scenario illustrates an effective type of frontal teaching:

The Real World

Standing at her desk in front of her second-grade class, Ms. Jaffe demonstrates how to roll *hallah* dough into long ropes. She then prompts her students to practice rolling out their own pieces of dough. She makes sure each student is able to roll out relatively uniform ropes, and she then demonstrates how to braid the ropes.

In this scenario, Ms. Jaffe uses *direct instruction,* a type of frontal teaching. In this model, the teacher demonstrates a skill, provides time for guided practice, and checks students' understanding. It is a good way to teach a variety of skills, including printing Hebrew letters, performing rituals, and creating art projects.

In contrast to frontal teaching is **group work,** or *cooperative-learning activities,* in which students gather in small groups and direct their own work. Group work is an ideal teaching method for religious schools because it fosters relationships among students who see one another only once or twice a week. In addition, slower students benefit from working with students who have a stronger grasp of the material, and more-advanced students gain from the deeper thinking they use to assist others. Students working in groups tend to develop ideas that they would not think of on their own.

Despite its many benefits, group work can be challenging. Some students may dominate a group while others hardly participate. Students may also bicker or fail to support one another's ideas. To promote cooperation, assign a role to each student in each group. Having the responsibility of leader, timekeeper, recorder, materials handler, reader, and presenter helps students feel like important members of their group.

Discussion-based lessons combine frontal teaching and group work. As in frontal teaching, the teacher directs the class, but in this model the students work together to reach an understanding of the material. Lessons may be *problem based,* with students working together to solve a problem—for example, an ethical dilemma, a Bible crossword puzzle, or placing historical events on a timeline. Problem-based discussions are particularly useful for the study of texts. Other lessons may be *sharing based,* with students reflecting on a shared experience, such as a field trip.

To prepare for a discussion-based lesson, write a variety of questions. Some should be simple, requiring students to recall information. For example, they might discuss whether they agree or disagree with a statement and explain why. For a lesson about the binding of Isaac, you might ask, "What did Isaac think would happen when he reached the top of Mount Moriah with his father? What in the text leads you to your conclusion?" Other questions should require students to compare and contrast ideas or think about how they would feel in a particular situation. For the same lesson, you might ask, "In your opinion, why did God command Abraham to sacrifice Isaac? Was Abraham right to listen to God? Is it ever acceptable to disobey God?" You can choose the questions you ask according to the direction the discussion takes. After asking a question, allow several seconds of "wait time" for students to recall the relevant information and formulate a response.

Finally, incorporate **individual seat work** into your lessons—for example, practicing reading Hebrew, reviewing worksheets, writing, and doing art projects. During seat-work time, you and your *madrich* or *madrichah* should walk around the room, observing students' work and offering help.

Focus on Text

בֶּן זוֹמָא אוֹמֵר, "אֵיזֶהוּ חָכָם? הַלּוֹמֵד מִכָּל אָדָם."

Ben Zoma said, "Who is wise? One who learns from all people."

—Pirkei Avot 4:1

This teaching from Pirkei Avot suggests that we can learn from everyone, including our students. During class discussions or while reviewing students' work, you may encounter insights that, while different from your own, are thoughtful and valid. By taking these ideas seriously and discussing them with the student or the class, you will show that you respect and value your students' opinions, and you will demonstrate the importance of learning from one another.

Describe an experience in your life in which you learned something from an unexpected source.

Reflections

In this workshop, you learned how to plan lessons that include a set induction, varied activities, assessment, and closure. You also learned how to use Understanding by Design to teach enduring understandings. List at least three insights you gained from this workshop that will help you prepare your lessons.

Managing the Jewish Classroom

Objectives

By the end of this workshop, you will be able to:

▶ Describe how creative lesson planning and a respectful classroom culture can help you manage your classroom.

▶ List at least two techniques for motivating students to stay on task, participate in class activities, complete their work, and behave properly.

▶ List and explain three ways in which to maintain discipline in the classroom.

▶ Explain how teaching with Jewish values can help you manage your class.

Lesson Launch

Read the following list of classroom management strategies. Then, rank the strategies from the one you consider most important (1) to the one you consider least important (7). Compare your rankings with those of other teachers in your group. Discuss how your ideas about classroom management are similar or different.

_____ Creating a culture of respect in the classroom.

_____ Having a clear discipline process, including warnings, time-outs, and calls home.

_____ Knowing your students well.

_____ Using a variety of teaching techniques to keep lessons engaging.

_____ Mastering a look or tone of voice that lets students know it is time to quiet down.

_____ Using rewards and punishments to motivate students.

_____ Promoting Jewish values in your classroom.

New teachers report that classroom management is one of the most difficult aspects of teaching. They need guidance to keep students engaged and on task and to keep them from behaving inappropriately.

The best way to manage your classroom effectively is to use a variety of strategies to motivate students, keep them focused, and help them feel like integral members of the classroom community. Remember: act confidently, even if you do not feel confident! In this workshop, you will learn how you can use good planning, interesting lessons, and a respectful classroom culture to maintain control. You will also learn specific techniques for managing misbehavior when it occurs despite your best proactive efforts.

CREATING A CULTURE OF RESPECT

Think of a teacher, employer, or friend whom you respect. Describe how that person earned your respect.

_____

_____

_____

_____

_____

Respect—in Hebrew, *kavod*—is an important Jewish value that is central to successful classroom management. Your students should trust you and believe that you care about them. In order to earn their respect, you must treat them with respect. In Workshop 1, we learned about things you can do to earn the respect of your students, for example, be friendly, but do not try to be your students' friend, and make only those promises that you can and will fulfill.

MOTIVATING STUDENTS

Another key to successful classroom management is motivating students to stay on task, participate in class activities, complete their work, and behave properly in the classroom. Often the best way to motivate students is to "catch them being good." Look for occasions to thank them for their participation in class, compliment their written work, or just give them a smile.

Physical rewards can also be motivating, as this scenario demonstrates:

The Real World

Ms. Levi, a fourth-grade teacher, knows it is important to review new material at the end of each class session, but her students are too distracted by the expectation of the bell to participate in a question-and-answer session. She has asked her *madrich*, Zach, to lead a blackboard baseball review game during the last ten minutes of class. The first week the students are too busy watching the clock to participate fully. Ms. Levi encourages Zach to try again with a different tactic: awarding stickers for correct answers. After a few weeks, the students excitedly await the game instead of the bell. Ms. Levi and Zach have motivated the students to participate in the review by offering a small reward.

The sticker reward system that Zach used motivates students to cooperate and contribute to class activities. Teachers may also encourage good behavior by rewarding the class with a pizza party. Some teachers award small prizes for books read or homework assignments completed. Some award "shekels" that can be cashed in once a month for prizes.

You can also reward students' cooperation—and initiative—by giving students a greater say in running the class. For example, you might let students choose the game they will play near the end of the class period, allow them to choose between two exercises in their textbook, or allocate time for them to teach a topic of their choice.

Sometimes a reward is built into an activity. For example, the enjoyment of playing a game is a reward in itself. Puzzles, art projects, and field trips have intrinsic rewards too. Your students' motivation to learn and succeed is also very important. Such motivation is highly personal, with students working to satisfy their need for success. By establishing clear milestones of success—for example, reading a Hebrew prayer with fewer than three mistakes—you can encourage students to pursue personal goals.

Rewards are not the only way to motivate students. Students will often comply with your requests in order to avoid negative consequences, such as missing recess or your calling their parents. Often a stern look from you is enough to stop students from talking out of turn or misbehaving. If that doesn't work, a discussion with the principal or a verbal or written warning may motivate a change in behavior. You can also use these techniques:

- ▶ *Give non-verbal cues* such as making eye contact, moving into the student's space, or flicking the lights on and off.
- ▶ *Take away a privilege* such as free time or a choice of seats.
- ▶ *Call the student's parent* if the behavior continues. Describe anecdotally the behavior you've observed and ask for the parent's help in controlling it.

To maintain the culture of respect, it is essential that you use the mildest punishment that will be effective and that you always avoid humiliating students.

You will sometimes have to motivate students to do things they do not want to do or are afraid to do. You may need to motivate a shy student to participate in an activity, quiet a talkative student during an assembly, or encourage a dispirited student to try again.

How might you respond to these challenges?

- ▶ Motivate a shy student to participate in a group role-playing activity:

  _____

  _____

  _____

▶ Quiet a talkative student during an assembly:

_____

_____

_____

▶ Encourage a dispirited student to try reading a Hebrew selection again:

_____

_____

_____

_____

Effective Teaching as a Strategy for Managing the Classroom

The best way to keep students on task is to practice effective teaching techniques. Researchers, including Edmund Emmer and Carolyn Evertson, authors of several books on classroom management, have found that effective teachers use the following strategies:

▶ **List on the board the tasks that students need to complete when they arrive in class.** For example: (1) Check off your name on the attendance poster; (2) put money in the tzedakah jar; (3) take an index card and on it write one thing from the previous week's lesson; (4) take a worksheet from the teacher's desk and complete the activity. Each week, some activities may be the same (the attendance and tzedakah procedures, for example), but others will vary.

▶ **Run the classroom efficiently, and manage behavior problems swiftly.** The most effective teachers handle discipline problems while allowing the rest of the class to continue working on the lesson. For example, if two students are chatting when they should be participating in a whole-class discussion, give them a warning look or approach their desks while continuing to lead the rest of the class in the discussion. Limit behaviors that interrupt the flow of activities and slow the momentum of a lesson.

▶ **Make sure students know what is expected of them, and monitor their progress.** Use assessments such as writing assignments, oral questions, quizzes, and presentations. Holding students accountable for their work helps keep them on task.

▶ **Give clear instructions and explanations in a variety of forms**—written, spoken, and demonstrated—so that students are able to participate fully without becoming confused or falling behind. When students feel inept or frustrated, they often misbehave. Plan lessons carefully. Vary teaching methods to appeal to students with different learning styles. For example, a lesson on King David might include studying a map, a small-group discussion, an activity in the textbook, and an art project or dramatic role-playing.

Based on your teaching situation (for example, grade level and curriculum), describe one way in which you can incorporate each of the strategies above into your teaching.

1. List procedures for start of class: _____

_____

2. Run the classroom efficiently: _____

_____

3. Provide clear objectives: _____

_____

4. Give clear instructions and explanations: _____

_____

MANAGING MISBEHAVIOR

Keeping students actively engaged in learning will help prevent most disruptive behavior. However, some students may misbehave in class—for example, by talking out of turn or distracting others—because they are bored, tired, falling behind, or distracted by personal problems. Knowing the cause of a student's misbehavior can help you decide which intervention strategy to use.

Regardless of the cause of a student's misbehavior, spotting it quickly and issuing a clear, firm directive to stop the behavior are the best first steps in dealing with a problem. From your own school days, you may remember teachers who seemed to have "eyes in the back of their head." Such teachers spot behavior problems quickly and move to control them before they escalate.

You can use a variety of interventions to deal with misbehavior. Among them are:

Nonverbal means of intervention: A variety of nonverbal strategies can help students regain their focus on classroom activities. Some educators use rhythm clapping: Clap out a short rhythm, and have students respond by repeating it. Other nonverbal techniques for refocusing the class's attention include flicking the classroom lights on and off, ringing a bell, and holding two fingers in the air. You can also use nonverbal techniques to manage an individual student's disruptive behavior—for example, move close to the student and make eye contact. This tactic allows you to maintain the momentum of the lesson while dealing with a student's misbehavior.

Rule-focused means of intervention: Rule-focused intervention focuses on stopping behaviors quickly and making sure students know what they did wrong. To use this strategy, quietly ask the student to stop the inappropriate behavior; then, maintain eye contact with the student until he or she corrects the behavior. Remind the student of the correct rule or procedure by referring to your classroom rules or list of Jewish values. You might say, for example, "Sarah, you are not showing *derech eretz*," or "Ethan, I like the way you demonstrated *kavod* when you helped Sarah play the flash-card game." This strategy is most effective in dealing with disruptions during group work or individual seat work, when you can talk to a student without interrupting the entire class. If you find that several students are off task, consider changing the activity to one that captures everyone's attention—for example, a challenging discussion or a content-rich game.

HINT: Try not to sweat the small stuff. If you understand normative behavior for the age group you teach and you don't overreact to it, you'll find that your class will run smoothly and pleasantly. But by all means take corrective action in response to behavior that disrupts the goals of your class.

Creating a Values-Based Classroom

It is especially appropriate in the religious school setting to promote student self-management by stressing socially just values. By making Jewish values a core part of your curriculum, you can steer your students toward making responsible choices about their behavior. As you learned in Workshop 1, incorporating *midot* (Jewish values) such as *derech eretz* and tzedakah into your regular classroom routine contributes to the creation of a caring community.

Read this list of Jewish values, and circle six that you will promote in your classroom.

- *derech eretz*
  (appropriate behavior)

- *kavod*
  (honor; respect)

- *tzedek*
  (justice)

- *gemilut ḥasadim*
  (acts of loving-kindness)

- *tikkun olam*
  (repair of the world)

- *ḥesed*
  (righteousness)

- *lo levayesh*
  (not embarrassing others)

- *klal Yisra'el*
  (Jewish unity)

- *talmud Torah* (study)

- *emet* (truth)

- *sh'lom bayit/sh'lom kitah*
  (peace in the home/peace in the classroom)

- *l'shon hara*
  (avoiding gossip)

Once you have identified the six Jewish values that you will focus on, read stories illustrating those values (ask your principal for suggestions), and have students role-play scenarios in which they must make decisions based on the values. Have students make a poster illustrating the six values, or have them make one poster for each value. Consistently reinforcing the importance of these *midot* will help your students make better choices about their behavior in your classroom. In addition to teaching *about* these values, teach *with* them.

Focus on Text

אָנֹכִי יְיָ אֱלֹהֶיךָ.

"I am Adonai your God..."

—Exodus 20: 2

Unlike the commandments that require specific actions such as keeping Shabbat and honoring one's parents, or prohibit specific actions such as murder and stealing, the first of the Ten Commandments states no rule governing behavior. It simply establishes God's authority ("I am Adonai your God").

1. In your opinion, why does the first commandment establish God's authority?

_____

_____

_____

2. Similarly, you should establish authority in your classroom. Why is this important?

_____

_____

_____

3. How will you go about establishing this authority? Which of the strategies and ideas that you have learned in this workshop will help you establish yourself as an authority figure?

_____

_____

_____

Reflections

Create two lists to guide your classroom management practices. In one, describe the things you plan to strive for in managing your classroom. In the other, describe the things that you want to avoid.

In managing my classroom
I will strive to . . .

In managing my classroom
I will avoid . . .

How Students Learn

Objectives

By the end of this workshop, you will be able to:

▶ Explain the difference between visual learners, auditory learners, and kinesthetic and tactile learners.

▶ Identify at least three characteristics of the age group with which you work.

▶ Describe at least two types of intelligence.

▶ Explain how you will use Bloom's Taxonomy to create lessons that require students to think at levels of varying complexity.

Lesson Launch

Circle the number that most accurately reflects your skills and preferences. On a scale of 1 to 5, 1 is not at all true for you, 3 is somewhat true, and 5 is very true.

	Not True—Somewhat True—Very True				
a. I can read maps easily.	1	2	3	4	5
b. I remember things better when I take notes.	1	2	3	4	5
c. I can draw well.	1	2	3	4	5
d. I am good at doing crossword puzzles.	1	2	3	4	5
e. I understand oral better than written directions.	1	2	3	4	5
f. I would rather hear a speaker than read an article.	1	2	3	4	5
g. I am articulate and enjoy discussions and debates.	1	2	3	4	5
h. I like to listen to the radio.	1	2	3	4	5
i. I enjoy physical activities.	1	2	3	4	5
j. I am good at working with my hands.	1	2	3	4	5
k. I would rather be active than read or watch a movie.	1	2	3	4	5

VISUAL LEARNERS

If you circled mostly 4's and 5's in response to items a–d, you are likely a visual learner: You learn by seeing. Visual learners are aided in understanding by viewing images such as illustrations, charts, and diagrams.

AUDITORY LEARNERS

If you circled mostly 4's and 5's in response to items e–h, you are likely an auditory learner: You learn by hearing. Auditory learners are aided in understanding by listening to people speaking or by listening to music.

KINESTHETIC AND TACTILE LEARNERS

If you circled mostly 4's and 5's in response to items i–k, you are likely a kinesthetic or tactile learner: You learn by moving or touching. Kinesthetic and tactile learners are aided in understanding by taking part in hands-on activities.

People vary widely in the ways in which they learn. In preparing lessons, you should try to include lessons that will appeal to visual, auditory, and kinesthetic and tactile learners. When teaching the *alef-bet,* for example, you might write the letters on the board (for visual learners), say the names and sounds of the letters (for auditory learners), and have students first cut the letters out of felt and place them on a felt board and then practice writing them (for kinesthetic and tactile learners). To maximize learning and long-term retention, it is best to expose students to all three forms of instruction.

Styles of learning are only one of many variables that affect the learning process. In this workshop, you will also discover how developmental stages and types of intelligence affect learning.

Stages of Development

Think back to your elementary school years, when you learned by hearing stories, singing songs, manipulating shapes, and drawing pictures. Now you probably learn by attending lectures, doing research on the Internet, visiting museums, and listening to recordings. How people learn changes a great deal with age. It is essential to tailor your teaching to the age of the students you are working with. Read the following developmental profiles. Then, complete the activity that follows.

Kindergarten: Five-Year-Olds . . .
are active and purposeful; are developing a consciousness of right and wrong but cannot always distinguish between them or accept responsibility; understand relationships in the context of family; vary greatly from one another in learning skills and physical abilities; have developed a sense of God's love and care by means of attention given to them by loving and caring adults; have short attention spans; can learn from mistakes; appreciate the help of others and want to help others; are beginning to wonder about life and death.

Grade 1: Six-Year-Olds . . .
are developing a sense of the world beyond home; are eager to learn; ask many questions; have a great imagination but little concept of time and space; find that their personal desires may conflict with their standards; feel a sense of responsibility to the group; have questions about God; want honest and immediate answers to their questions.

Grade 2: Seven-Year-Olds . . .
are becoming introspective; are sensitive to adult approval; are self-critical; are richly imaginative but interested in the here and now; care about fair play and honesty; are beginning to understand the meaning of prayer; show an interest in Bible heroes; are developing a sense of community beyond home and school; assimilate new information when it is presented in terms of familiar examples.

Grade 3: Eight-Year-Olds . . .
are aware of physical and intellectual growth; are impatient to get started on new projects but eager to finish; wish to do things their way but still crave adult approval and support; are becoming better communicators but may talk for the sake of talking; enjoy collecting and swapping; may be interested in dramatics; find meaning in time and space; like groups; uphold rules; can understand the personal relationship to God as related to God's caring for others.

Grade 4: Nine-Year-Olds . . .

have a longer attention span and therefore greater independence than younger children; want to be accepted as responsible yet recognize their need for help; are likely to attach themselves to role models; may not have a sense of their limitations; highly value fair play and individual rights; are thinking more clearly about right and wrong; are curious about the unknown and find the past exciting; can build on previous knowledge; vary greatly from one another in their reading skills; consider their teacher an important leader and opinion maker; may be guided by the Bible's lessons in their moral development; favor facts and people over fantasy and abstract ideas.

Grade 5: Ten-Year-Olds . . .

are experiencing a period of preadolescent adjustment; are widening their interests; may have difficulty conceptualizing or generalizing but are developing memorization skills; have evolved a sense of time that is conducive to the study of history; have interests specific to their sex; need reinforcement of the dos and don'ts of living in society; may have deep religious feelings and a close relationship with God; may have questions about the concept of faith; know and can apply many facts of Jewish history and observance.

Grade 6: Eleven-Year-Olds . . .

are eager to discover secrets; want to figure out ethical and religious matters for themselves; differ by sex, with girls typically developing physically and emotionally more rapidly than boys; are increasingly sensitive to criticism; are capable of strong feelings (anger, fear, dejection, elation); are increasingly capable of abstract thinking; are finding relationships with peers both exciting and painful; are likely to be critical of adults; are open to more mature values but wish to discover them by themselves; see a connection between religious teaching and personal problems.

Grade 7: Twelve-Year-Olds . . .

differ in intellectual and physical development, with girls leading boys by about a year; with guidance can see the relationship between events; are resentful of repetitive, childish activity; are beginning to search for a philosophy of life; can be encouraged to express abstract values; are receptive to social-action projects; enjoy responsibilities that elicit a sense of achievement.

Use the information about learning styles and stages of development to discuss these questions:

1. At what age do children develop interests specific to their sex?

2. What age or ages are characterized by imaginative thought?

3. At what age do children desire greater independence?

4. At what age or ages would children be most interested in learning about Abraham's journey to Canaan?

5. At what age or ages would students most enjoy collecting and trading Israeli stamps?

Assign to the following items the grade level at which students typically first exhibit the characteristic:

_____ has a growing sense of the world beyond home

_____ understands relationships in the context of family

_____ finds relationships with peers both exciting and painful

_____ needs reinforcement of the dos and don'ts of living in society

_____ may become attached to role models

Describe two similarities and two differences between first-graders and second-graders:

Similarities: _____

_____

Differences: _____

_____

How are the students you are teaching likely to relate to God?

_____

_____

_____

Multiple Intelligences

Linguistic Intelligence / WORD SMART

Displays an understanding of the meaning and order of words. Writers and poets exhibit linguistic intelligence.

Logical or Mathematical Intelligence / NUMBERS SMART

Has strong abilities in math and other complex logical systems, as well as scientific ability. Researchers, businesspeople, and doctors display logical or mathematical intelligence.

Musical Intelligence / MUSIC SMART

Has the ability to understand and create music. Musicians, composers, and singers have musical intelligence.

Visual or Spatial Intelligence / PICTURE SMART

Has the ability to think in pictures, to create a mental image of the world. Painters, architects, sculptors, and designers demonstrate visual or spatial intelligence.

Bodily-Kinesthetic Intelligence / BODY SMART

Has the ability to express oneself or achieve a goal by using the body skillfully. Mimes, dancers, basketball players, and actors are among those who display bodily-kinesthetic intelligence.

Interpersonal Intelligence / PEOPLE SMART

Has the ability to perceive and understand others—their moods, desires, and motivations. Political and religious leaders, parents and teachers, and therapists use interpersonal intelligence.

Intrapersonal Intelligence / MYSELF SMART

Has an understanding of own emotions. Many novelists and counselors use their own experiences to influence, enlighten, or guide others.

Naturalist Intelligence / NATURE SMART

Has the ability to identify and classify patterns, especially in the natural world. Scientists, biologists, and anthropologists have high naturalist intelligence.

The theory of multiple intelligences is particularly valuable when students are struggling with a concept or skill. Think about connecting the material to words, numbers, pictures, music, movement, a social experience, or a personal reflection. For example, if students are learning the blessing over the Ḥanukkah candles, you might have them explore the meaning of each word, put the scrambled words of the blessings in order, practice reciting the blessings while lighting the candles, sing the blessings together, or recite the blessings privately while thinking about their own Ḥanukkah experiences. You do not need to use all of these strategies in every lesson, but do try to vary the strategies you use so that you reach students with every type of intelligence.

To practice this technique, choose one of the following concepts, and create a grade level appropriate activity that appeals to each of the eight intelligences. Circle the topic you have chosen to work with.

- ► the mitzvah of giving tzedakah
- ► the events of the Purim story
- ► the major cities of Israel

Linguistic: _____

_____

Logical or mathematical: _____

_____

Musical: _____

_____

Visual or spatial: _____

_____

Bodily-kinesthetic: _____

_____

Interpersonal: _____

_____

Intrapersonal: _____

_____

Naturalist: _____

_____

BLOOM'S TAXONOMY

In this workshop, you have explored how different students learn differently. However, students are also alike in the way they learn. For example, all students process information on a variety of cognitive levels, from the simple recall of facts to the more complex evaluation of ideas.

In 1956, a group of educational psychologists led by Benjamin Bloom found that over 95 percent of test questions required students to function at only the most simple cognitive levels: factual recall and comprehension. The following chart, known as Bloom's Taxonomy, encourages teachers to ask questions and assign activities that push students to think at more complex cognitive levels.

Level or Competence	Definition or Skills Observed	Key Instruction or Question Words	Example
Knowledge	Students recall information as it was presented to them.	define, tell, label, name	List Maimonides' eight levels of tzedakah.
Comprehension	Students understand information, interpret facts, and transform knowledge into new contexts.	paraphrase, interpret, explain, illustrate	Explain why helping a person become self-supporting represents the highest form of tzedakah.
Application	Students use knowledge to complete a new problem or task.	use, solve, demonstrate, apply	Read the following examples of tzedakah. On which level of the tzedakah ladder does each example fit?
Analysis	Students classify or compare and contrast information.	categorize, compare, contrast, arrange	Compare and contrast the third level of tzedakah, in which the donor is anonymous, and the fourth level, in which the receiver is anonymous. What are the benefits of each?
Synthesis	Students originate ideas, predict outcomes, and draw conclusions.	create, plan, hypothesize, invent	Create a plan for a tzedakah project that involves one of the three highest levels of tzedakah.
Evaluation	Students assess, appraise, and critique information and ideas.	test, measure, judge, critique	Describe a type of giving that you might add to Maimonides' ladder of tzedakah. Would you change the order in any way?

Choose a topic that you will be teaching in the upcoming weeks. Using Bloom's Taxonomy as a guide, describe activities that would illustrate each of its levels.

Topic: _____

Knowledge: _____

_____

Comprehension: _____

_____

Application: _____

_____

Analysis: _____

_____

Synthesis: _____

_____

Evaluation: _____

_____

Focus on Text

כְּנֶגֶד אַרְבָּעָה בָנִים דִּבְּרָה תוֹרָה: אֶחָד חָכָם וְאֶחָד רָשָׁע וְאֶחָד תָּם וְאֶחָד שֶׁאֵינוֹ יוֹדֵעַ לִשְׁאוֹל.

The Torah tells us about four different children: one who is wise and one who is wicked and one who is simple and one who does not know how to ask.

—Passover Haggadah

Who are these four children described in the Haggadah? One interpretation is that they are children with different learning abilities. The wise child is scholarly, wanting to know as much as possible. The wicked child is skeptical and disengaged from learning. The simple child is interested in or capable of learning only the most basic information. The one who does not know how to ask may be shy or a slow learner.

Choose one of the children mentioned in the Hagaddah, and describe him or her more extensively. Without mentioning names, draw on your experience with one or more of the students in your class.

_____

_____

_____

The children described in the Hagaddah may also be seen as being at different stages of development. The one who does not know how to ask might be a baby. The simple child is perhaps a preschool or elementary-school student. The wicked child may be an adolescent struggling to define himself or herself as an individual distinct from parents and community. The wise child may be of college age, eager to discover what the world has to offer.

Give an example of how you might tailor a lesson to the developmental level of your students.

_____

_____

_____

Reflections

Complete the following sentences:

1. At the beginning of the workshop, I identified my own learning style as _____.

2. As a teacher, I need to compensate for my learning style by focusing especially on _____ learners. I can do this by including these types of activities or teaching strategies:

   a. _____

   b. _____

   c. _____

Teaching Students with Learning Differences

Objectives

By the end of this workshop, you will be able to:

▶ Describe inattention, hyperactivity, and impulsivity caused by attention deficit hyperactivity disorder (ADHD).

▶ List at least three techniques for reaching students with disabilities.

▶ Explain how you can remove some of the stumbling blocks from mainstream classrooms.

Lesson Launch

Do you have students in your class who have been diagnosed with ADHD? Do you have students who have more trouble staying seated and on task than other students? If so, what behaviors do they tend to exhibit? In the space below, describe the behaviors of those students.

_____

_____

_____

_____

In this chapter, you will learn what defines ADHD and other learning differences. You will also learn strategies for helping students with learning disabilities succeed in your class.

Learning Disabilities

A learning disability (LD) is a neurological disorder that hinders the understanding and use of spoken or written language. An LD might cause a student to struggle with listening, concentrating, reading, writing, or spelling, or with organizational skills. Students diagnosed with an LD can learn strategies that help them manage it, and teachers can learn strategies for assisting them.

ADHD

Attention deficit hyperactivity disorder (ADHD) is a common learning disability: It is estimated that 3 to 5 percent of children have ADHD, so in a class of twenty students, at least one child might be affected. Teachers should have a basic understanding of ADHD so that they can better assist children affected by it. The disorder is characterized by three symptoms: inattention, hyperactivity, and impulsivity.

> ▶ **Inattention.** Students who are inattentive have a hard time focusing. During class, they may be distracted by peripheral sights and sounds—for example, by people passing in the hallway or activity they observe through the window. They find it difficult to complete assignments or engage in an activity for more than a few minutes.

> ▶ **Hyperactivity.** Students who are hyperactive seem to be in motion all the time. They get out of their chair to walk around the room or play with whatever is in sight, or they squirm when seated. They often lack organizational skills. In addition, they may talk when the class is expected to be quiet.

> ▶ **Impulsivity.** Students who are impulsive find it hard to wait their turn and frequently blurt out responses before a teacher finishes asking a question.

Not everyone who demonstrates these symptoms has ADHD. In fact, most students exhibit such behaviors once in a while. To be diagnosed with ADHD, a child must demonstrate all three symptoms continually for at least six months. The symptoms must be excessive for the child's age and must create a hardship in at least two areas of his or her life—for example, on the playground and at friends' homes.

Strategies for Teaching Students with ADHD

The following are useful strategies for working with students with ADHD.

▶ **Incorporate movement.** Whenever possible, allow students to get up out of their seats. Sending students with ADHD on small errands to the office or asking them to pass out supplies provides them with a chance to move around while making them feel important.

▶ **Use cues.** To focus a student's attention on a task, use eye contact or physical cues such as a gentle touch on the arm or shoulder. If one of your students leaves the room for tutoring, you might work out a private signal, such as folding your arms, to let a student know that it is time to meet with the tutor. This strategy makes the tutoring seem special rather than a cause for embarrassment.

▶ **Break projects into small, manageable steps.** Give short, easy-to-understand instructions. Be flexible about the amount of time in which a project must be completed, but don't let your students off the hook. It is important to hold *all* students accountable while making necessary modifications.

▶ **Provide organizational tools.** Offer checklists and labels. Help students label their papers and organize their desks to reduce distractions. Seat students with ADHD away from the door and windows to further minimize distractions.

▶ **Administer discipline with care.** Give ADHD students a way to cope with their impulsive urges. For example, allow them to wander around the room, hang something on the bulletin board, or manage a chart. Do not punish behaviors that are symptoms of the child's ADHD. However, you should discipline any negative behaviors that are not related to the learning disability, such as cheating or acting unkindly. Set boundaries in a clear and caring way. Be consistent in articulating and enforcing those boundaries.

▶ **Provide individual attention.** *Madrichim* can provide one-on-one help and guidance for students who take extra time to complete their work, have difficulty focusing, or need help understanding assignments. Before assigning a *madrich* or *madrichah* to work with students with LDs, talk to him or her about the students' needs. You might also have your assistant read this chapter or the chapter on special needs in *The Madrichim Manual*.

▶ **Give positive reinforcement.** Reward students' success with stickers, points on a chart, and verbal praise.

▶ **Be objective.** Do not be offended if a student with ADHD becomes distracted during a lesson. The behavior is not a reflection of your skills as a teacher but a manifestation of the disorder.

▶ **Take medication into consideration.** If students in your class take medication, it is helpful to know when they take it and how it affects them. For example, some medications make children sleepy. If you know that one of your students is taking such a medication, you will understand the reason for his or her lethargy.

Put It into Practice: Managing Students with ADHD

Discuss the steps you would take to remedy the following situations. Record your ideas on the lines provided.

1. You suspect that a student in your class has ADHD, but there is no mention of a diagnosis in his or her file. With the best interests of the student *and* the class in mind, describe steps you might take.

_____

_____

_____

2. Your students are working in small groups to prepare for a model Passover seder. A student with ADHD keeps jumping up and playing with decorations on the walls. What can you do to help him or her focus on the group's work?

_____

_____

_____

OTHER LEARNING CHALLENGES

There are a variety of disabilities that cause learning problems, such as visual and auditory processing difficulties, Tourette's syndrome, Down syndrome, and autism. If a student in your class has one of these differences, work with your principal and the student's parent to create a plan for his or her success in your classroom. Find out what strategies have worked for the child's secular school teachers and previous religious school teachers. Ask your principal about modifying assignments and/ or assigning a *madrich* or *madrichah* to sit with the student in your classroom.

Working with Parents

Remember that your students' parents are your partners in their children's Jewish education. If you know that a child has learning differences, talk to the child's parent about the strategies that have worked well for the child in other situations. Find out what the child's secular school is doing to assist in the child's success. If the student has difficulty completing work in the time allotted in class, ask the parent to help the child complete the work at home.

Focus on Text

לֹא־תְקַלֵּל חֵרֵשׁ וְלִפְנֵי עִוֵּר לֹא תִתֵּן מִכְשֹׁל.

You shall not insult the deaf or place a stumbling block before the blind.

—Leviticus 19:14

Tradition teaches that this verse refers to all who lack awareness or ability. Putting students with learning disabilities in a classroom in which they cannot succeed is like putting a stumbling block before the blind. For example, students with learning disabilities often struggle with time limits. You might have a *madrich* or *madrichah* take the student aside to allow the student more time to complete a project while the rest of the class moves on to another activity.

Students with learning disabilities may feel frustrated, anxious, and tense in a mainstream classroom. Students with processing delays, for example, can be easily tripped up by having to consider the teacher's questions and come up with an answer while the rest of the class waits. You can remove this stumbling block by calling on a student you know has a processing disorder only when the student signals that he or she is prepared to answer the question.

Time and anxiety are only two of the stumbling blocks that students with learning disabilities face. Students with ADHD may be distracted by the sights and sounds of the classroom. Students with dyslexia may have trouble adjusting to the fact that Hebrew is read from right to left. Students who take medication may feel the effects wearing off during an afternoon class. Talk to these students about what they consider to be the stumbling blocks in your class and what you can do to remove them. Remember that these students deal with the same obstacles in secular school and have probably developed techniques to help them cope.

Describe the stumbling blocks that students might face in your class.

_____

_____

_____

_____

_____

Remember that every student has unique learning needs. Some students need to be challenged more than others; some are shy and have difficulty working in groups; some need more time to process verbal instructions. Try to understand the learning needs of each of your students.

Reflections

Imagine a classroom specially designed to help students with LDs and students without LDs learn together in the most effective way possible. How would you create a lesson about Shabbat that would appeal to both types of students? What would the students learn? What activities would they engage in? Write your lesson plan here.

Lesson Plan

Workshop 6

Conclusion

חֲנֹךְ לַנַּעַר עַל־פִּי דַרְכּוֹ גַּם כִּי־יַזְקִין לֹא־יָסוּר מִמֶּנָּה׃

*Educate children in the way they should go,
and even when they are old, they will not depart from it.*

—Proverbs 22.6

In this handbook, you have explored ways to teach Jewish lessons that will last a lifetime. You have learned how to teach with Jewish values, how to include the entire family in Jewish learning, and how to create meaningful lessons that reach a diverse group of learners.

By accepting the position of Jewish teacher, you have chosen to become part of a community that is striving to make Judaism meaningful for the next generation. As you go forward, use the lessons you have learned in this course—and in the course of your life—to pass on to your students Jewish teachings, practices, and values.

May you continue to grow in your role!